R is for Risen

written by Crystal Bowman & Teri McKinley
pictures by Jacqueline L. Nuñez

Tyndale House Publishers
Carol Stream, Illinois

Dedicated to Aria and McKenna—
May you know the love and joy of our risen Savior.

The journey of creating this book has felt unique from the beginning.
In recognition, we'd like to acknowledge those who helped make it possible.

With special thanks—
To Anthony for being the inspiration behind the alphabet words
and all your support in writing this story.
To Debbie King and the Tyndale team for your excellence
and partnering with us to plant seeds of truth in young hearts and minds.
And most of all, to the Risen One whose victory over sin and death
gives eternal life to everyone who believes.

Visit Tyndale's website for kids at tyndale.com/kids.

Visit Crystal Bowman's website at crystalbowman.com.

Tyndale is a registered trademark of Tyndale House Ministries. The Tyndale Kids logo is a trademark of Tyndale House Ministries.

R Is for Risen: An ABC Easter Story

Copyright © 2025 by Crystal Bowman and Teri McKinley. All rights reserved.

Illustrations by Jacqueline L. Nuñez. Copyright © Tyndale House Publishers. All rights reserved.

Designed by Jacqueline L. Nuñez

Edited by Deborah King

Scripture quotations marked NLT are taken from the *Holy Bible*, New Living Translation, copyright © 1996, 2004, 2015 by Tyndale House Foundation. Used by permission of Tyndale House Publishers, Carol Stream, Illinois 60188. All rights reserved.

Scripture quotations marked GW are taken from *GOD'S WORD*®, copyright © 1995 by God's Word to the Nations. Used by permission of God's Word Mission Society. All rights reserved.

Scripture quotations marked NIrV are taken from the Holy Bible, *New International Reader's Version,*® NIrV.® Copyright © 1995, 1996, 1998, 2014 by Biblica, Inc.® Used by permission. All rights reserved worldwide.

Scripture quotations marked ICB are taken from the International Children's Bible®. Copyright © 1986, 1988, 1999 by Thomas Nelson. Used by permission. All rights reserved.

Published in association with the literary agency of Credo Communications, LLC, Grand Rapids, Michigan, credocommunications.net.

For manufacturing information regarding this product, please call 1-855-277-9400.

For information about special discounts for bulk purchases, please contact Tyndale House Publishers at csresponse@tyndale.com, or call 1-855-277-9400.

Library of Congress Cataloging-in-Publication Data

A catalog record for this book is available from the Library of Congress.

ISBN 978-1-4964-8729-2

Printed in China

31	30	29	28	27	26	25
7	6	5	4	3	2	1

How to Use This Book

Jesus' resurrection is an exciting story of victory that we celebrate every year at Easter. During his three-year ministry on earth, Jesus healed the sick, calmed the seas, and called people to follow him. Jesus explained to his followers ahead of time what was going to happen to him, but they did not understand what he meant until everything happened the way he said it would.

As you read this picture book with your children, they will learn all about the story of Easter—from Jesus riding on a donkey through the streets of Jerusalem to the joy and celebration of the empty tomb. The story is told in chronological order to help young minds understand why Jesus had to die and how he came back to life as our risen Savior. Following the alphabet letter by letter, children will see the events surrounding Jesus' death and resurrection unfold before their eyes. Bible verses are included with every letter to show where the events or prophecies can be found in Scripture. For additional insight, you can look up the verses with your children and read more of the Easter story in your Bible. Encourage your children to ask questions as you look for answers together.

We hope you and your family enjoy using this book to focus on the true meaning of Easter—that God sent his Son to earth to save us from sin and to be our Lord and Savior.

Crystal Bowman and Teri McKinley

A is for Arrived

Jesus came to Jerusalem.
People were everywhere.
He ARRIVED with his disciples.
Excitement filled the air.

*When they came near Jerusalem, . . .
Jesus sent two of his disciples ahead of him.*
Mark 11:1, GW

B is for Branches

A crowd stood by the roadside.
They laid their BRANCHES down.
They shouted out, "Hosanna!
Our king has come to town!"

*Many people spread their coats on the road.
Others spread branches they had cut in the fields.*

Mark 11:8, NIrV

C is for Colt

Jesus rode a donkey's COLT
along the road that day.
A prophet many years before
said it would be that way.

*Your king is coming to you.
. . . He is on the colt of a donkey.*
Zechariah 9:9, ICB

D is for Dinner

Jesus said, "Go into town.
It's time that you prepare
our special DINNER for tonight.
A man will meet you there."

[They] went into the city and found everything just as Jesus had said, and they prepared the Passover meal there.

Mark 14:16, NLT

E is for Eat

Jesus thanked his Father
before he broke the bread.
"This is my broken body.
Take it and EAT," he said.

*"Take this bread and eat it.
This bread is my body."*

Matthew 26:26, ICB

F is for Feet

Jesus washed his disciples' FEET
to show them what to do.
He said, "Go serve the ones you meet
the way that I served you."

*"I, your Lord and Teacher, have washed your feet.
So you also should wash one another's feet."*
John 13:14, NIrV

G is for Gethsemane

The disciples followed Jesus

to a place not far away.

The garden of GETHSEMANE

is where they stopped to pray.

Jesus went with the disciples to a place called Gethsemane.
He said to them, "Stay here while I go over there and pray."
Matthew 26:36, GW

H is for Heart

Jesus' HEART was very sad.
He knew he had to die.
"Abba, Father," Jesus prayed.
An angel heard his cry.

*[Jesus] said to them, "I am full of sorrow.
My heart is breaking with sadness."*
Mark 14:34, ICB

I is for I Am

Some soldiers came to the garden.
Their lanterns helped them see.
"Where is Jesus of Nazareth?"
Jesus said, "I AM he."

*When Jesus said, "I am he,"
they moved back.*

John 18:6, NIrV

J is for Jesus

Even though he never sinned
and always did what's right,
JESUS let them tie his hands
and didn't try to fight.

*[Jesus] willingly gave his life.
He was treated like a criminal.*

Isaiah 53:12, ICB

K is for King

The Roman governor questioned,
"Jesus, are you a KING?"
"My kingdom is in heaven," he said.
"The truth is what I bring."

*Jesus answered, "You say that I am a king. That is true.
I was born for this: to tell people about the truth."*
John 18:37, ICB

L is for Led

The soldiers LED the Lord away.
"Hail to the King!" they said.
They twisted thorns to make a crown
and placed it on his head.

*The soldiers led Jesus away
into the palace.*
Mark 15:16, NIrV

M is for Marched

They made him drag a wooden cross.
He MARCHED the dusty road.
Simon was chosen from the crowd
to lift his heavy load.

On their way out of the city, they met a man from Cyrene.
His name was Simon. They forced him to carry the cross.
Matthew 27:32, NIrV

N is for Nails

With NAILS in Jesus' hands and feet,
the cross was lifted high.
"It is finished," Jesus said,
as people watched him die.

*They nailed [Jesus]
to the cross.*

Mark 15:24, NIrV

O is for Only

Jesus came from heaven to earth—
God's one and ONLY Son.
He did what no one else could do;
he died for everyone.

*God so loved the world
that he gave his one and only Son.*
John 3:16, NIrV

P is for Pilate

PILATE sent some Roman guards
to seal the tomb up tight.
They stood beside the giant stone
to watch it day and night.

*Pilate said, "Take some soldiers
and go guard the tomb the best way you know."*
Matthew 27:65, ICB

Q is for Quake

The ground began to QUAKE and shake
early in the day.
An angel came from heaven
and rolled the stone away.

*There was a powerful earthquake. An angel of the Lord
came down from heaven. . . . He rolled back the stone.*

Matthew 28:2, NIrV

R is for Risen

Women brought spices to the tomb.
"He's alive!" the angel said.
The women ran to tell the news:
"He's RISEN from the dead!"

*He is not here! He has risen,
just as he said he would!*

Matthew 28:6, NIrV

S is for Savior

Jesus is the SAVIOR
the world had waited for.
He came to be our Lord and King
and reign forevermore.

*God has brought one of David's descendants
to Israel to be their Savior. That descendant is Jesus.*

Acts 13:23, ICB

T is for Tomb

When John and Peter reached the TOMB,
the door was open wide.
But Jesus' body wasn't there
when they looked inside.

*[They] went into the tomb
and saw the strips of linen lying there.*
John 20:6, ICB

U is for Understand

The disciples finally saw the Lord.

He met them face-to-face.

His words helped them to UNDERSTAND

all that had taken place.

*[Jesus] opened their minds so
they could understand the Scriptures.*

Luke 24:45, NIrV

V is for Victory

Jesus gives the VICTORY
to all who trust his name.
He paid the price for sin and death.
That is why he came.

Let us give thanks to God! He gives us the victory because of what our Lord Jesus Christ has done.

1 Corinthians 15:57, NIrV

W is for World

Jesus told his followers,
"Tell everyone about me.
I'll be coming back someday
for all the WORLD to see."

*[Jesus] said to them, "Go into all the world.
Preach the good news to everyone."*

Mark 16:15, NIrV

X is for Exactly

Jesus did the work of God
EXACTLY as God planned.
Then he went back to heaven
to sit at God's right hand.

*I brought glory to you here on earth
by completing the work you gave me to do.*

John 17:4, NLT

Y is for You

Jesus is alive today.
He reigns with God above.
He gave his life so YOU could live
because of his great love.

*We know what real love is because
Jesus gave up his life for us.*
1 John 3:16, NLT

Z is for A and Z

Jesus is the Risen One,
our Savior and our Friend.
Jesus is the A AND Z,
the beginning and the end.

*I am the A and the Z, the first and the last,
the beginning and the end.*

Revelation 22:13, GW

 # About the Authors

CRYSTAL BOWMAN is a former preschool teacher and an award-winning, bestselling author. She has written more than 100 books for children, women, and families. She is also a lyricist, national speaker, and writing coach for children's writers. More than three million copies of her books have sold internationally, with many of them becoming CBA bestsellers. Her books have been translated into more than a dozen languages.

She has written numerous magazine articles, teacher resources, and Bible study materials. She is a regular contributor to *Clubhouse Jr.* magazine and has also contributed to several nonfiction women's compilation books. She has written two dozen books for the I Can Read! brand (Zonderkidz) and is one of the authors of the bestselling Little Blessings series (Tyndale Kids). She has also written for many popular series such as the Berenstain Bears, BOZ the Bear, and the Princess Parables. She and her daughter, Teri McKinley, launched the brand Our Daily Bread for Kids (Discovery House Publishers) and continue to develop more products for young children. Crystal and her husband enjoy spending time with their adult children and eight huggable grandkids.

As a mother of two young children, **TERI MCKINLEY** is passionate about helping kids understand God's love for them. She is an award-winning, bestselling author of more than a dozen books for children. Her books have been published in eight languages and have reached a wide variety of audiences. She is the coauthor and cocreator of the Our Daily Bread for Kids and Our Daily Bread for Little Hearts series. Some of her most celebrated titles include *M Is for Manger*, *A Is for Ark*, and *My Arms Will Hold You Tight*.

Teri's love for writing began in early childhood, as she often wrote short stories for fun. She was exposed to the publishing industry at a young age as the daughter of renowned children's author Crystal Bowman. Her love for writing grew as she attended book signings and writing conferences with her mom. Her first published works included magazine articles and greeting cards. Today Teri also enjoys writing for mothers and is continuing to grow projects to minister to them. Above all, Teri's heart is that her readers would be encouraged and brought closer to Christ through her writing.